AT THE
YEOMAN'S HOUSE

Ronald Blythe

AT THE
YEOMAN'S HOUSE

ENITHARMON PRESS

First published in 2011
by Enitharmon Press
26B Caversham Road
London NW5 2DU

www.enitharmon.co.uk

Distributed in the UK by
Central Books
99 Wallis Road
London E9 5LN

Distributed in the USA and Canada
by Dufour Editions Inc.
PO Box 7, Chester Springs
PA 19425, USA

ISBN: 978-1-904634-88-1 (hardback)
ISBN: 978-1-907587-17-7 (signed limited edition)

Enitharmon Press gratefully acknowledges the
financial support of Arts Council England.

Thanks are also due to Larissa Attisso and Peter Target for preparing
Ronald Blythe's text for typesetting; to Jennifer Camilleri, Picture Library
Administrator at the Royal Academy, for enabling us to use a reproduction
of John Nash's painting on the front cover; to Richard and Hattie Bawden
for the use of Richard's watercolour of Bottengoms Farm, and to
Brian Dicks for photographing it.

British Library Cataloguing-in-Publication Data.
A catalogue record for this book is available
from the British Library.

Designed in Albertina by Libanus Press
and printed in England by
Antony Rowe Ltd

CONTENTS

The Intruders   11

The Siting   19

Survival   37

Down to the Dwelling House   42

The See-Saw of Existence   45

Floors   53

Matrimony During the Building of the House   61

The Progress   67

The Dwindling   77

Family Circles   91

The Flowers of My Fields   105

June, Nine p.m.   122

In memoriam my parents

'Here is the ancient floor,
Footworn and hollowed and thin,
Here was the former door
Where the dead feet walked in.'

from Thomas Hardy's poem 'The Self-Unseeing'

THE INTRUDERS

NOT LONG AFTER THE WAR MOST OF WHAT WILLIAM Hazlitt called 'friends for life' were drawn into my solitude, for this is what it seemed at the time. It was like pulling some threads in a workbox and bringing out a tangle of unsuspected objects. I was working in a public library at that moment, writing poems and short stories, and running a literary society, but essentially lost. And then a tall woman in W.V.S uniform asked me for a miniature score of Mozart's *Idomeneo*. She ran it close to her smoked glasses, opening it here and there, humming a line or two. She was the artist Christine Kühlenthal, wife of John Nash. She came again the following day. 'You know our friends Cedric and Lett?' These were Sir Cedric Morris and his partner Lett Haines. The poet James Turner had introduced me to them that summer. He was teaching them to grow mushrooms in their dark barn. They had established the East Anglian School of Drawing and Painting at Benton End, an outsize yeoman's house which loomed above the River Brett at Hadleigh. Cedric was a fascinating plantsman, Lett an amazing cook. Painting was alfresco in this dry corner of Suffolk and their garden was spiky with easels. The house had Newlyn blue doors and reeked

Sir Cedric Morris when RB first met him, Benton End, Hadleigh, 1948

of wine and candles. It was Provence, or even Paris, in Suffolk. They had taught Lucien Freud and were to teach Maggi Hambling, a local girl. 'A writer,' they said, 'write our catalogues!' So I knew the Nashes' friends at Benton End, and thus I walked down the track to Bottengoms Farm. It would have been the spring of 1947.

A yeoman was above a farmer and lower than a gentleman, said William Cobbett. He was the independent master of a small estate, and both Bottengoms Farm and Benton End had remained small – and masterful. Their new artist owners were familiar travellers along the lanes which separated them, usually carrying plants, hardly ever pictures. There was surprisingly little literature on the sixteenth- and seventeenth-century outbreak of yeoman-house building, although these virtually indestructible dwellings were everywhere. Rowland Parker, in his *The Common Stream*, was almost alone in his account of what he called 'the great rebuild-ing', suggesting that it may have been due to 'the compounded result of expanding commerce, firm government, new ideas, a new outlook embracing wider horizons, renewed energy, pride in achievement and a spirit of sturdy independence.' In my novel *The Assassin* I imagined a gentleman's bewilderment when a yeoman had the nerve to build such a house within yards of his hall. But often they were built in the village street as much as in a remote dell like Bottengoms Farm.

I was born in such a house, with the village pump, vicarage, shop and school nearby. It was shaggily thatched, with a brick-lined well and double-seated privy behind it, pigsties at the corner, a sullen horse-pond and a pink wash all over it. Grandmother's Vicarage Cottage was a few steps away. The yeoman's fields could have been miles away. He could have been a Tudor commuter. Like Bottengoms, the agricultural depression had shoved my birthplace into the ignominious state of a double-dweller but

Bottengoms Farm, 1950

had this not been so a dividing paling would not have been moved so that I could crawl to my first neighbour, an old lady called Mrs Pleasants, and not experienced that still interior of warmth and few possessions, or had a ride in her pony and trap. She would have known my father when he was a baby.

My parents were twenty-two when I was born. My father had fought at Gallipoli in the 5th Suffolks and my mother had been a V.A.D. nurse in Bloomsbury. They had sped along two avenues in the vicar's brougham when they married on 1st August 1920. White ribbons were tied to the door handles and the whip. Mother remembered all the summer flowers, particularly the willow-herb. Be that as it may, as Mrs Pleasants could have said, we were upstarts in the yeoman's house, as indeed was she. We came of a long line of Suffolk shepherds. Many years after this – after another war, long after we had left it – it burnt down. I would see its immense chimney standing up in our garden like

Country children between the wars: Harold, Bernard, Constance and Ronald Blythe on the top meadow, Chilton, Suffolk

an orange tooth among the greengage trees. Eventually the site was covered in bungalows, plus one of those elevated signs which give the visitor a bit of local history. In this instance a carving of Sir Robert de Bures' brass in the church, the second best, we claimed, in England. 'Please, please', the Nashes would beseech me, when they went off to fill the sketchbooks for the winter painting, 'do be careful about fire!' All that paraffin, all that sparky wood, not to mention all those fags. No need for their fears for a yeoman-house-trained boy, non-smoking, virtuous of course. They would sometimes telephone from Cornwall – the china-clay country – or the Gower coast, smelling charred beams on the line. 'I meant to tell you, darling, to eat up that salt beef.'

RB at Bottengoms, 1978, photographed by Charles Hall

THE SITING

THERE ARE FARMS WHICH APPEAR TO HAVE GROWN furtively along the wasteland beyond the manor like a bit of edible fungus on the main family tree. I suspect that mine was here ages before the Normans came but was found not worth absorption. A man roofed-in a spring and dwelt beside it. The water supply still ran across the brick floor when I was a boy, as it had done for centuries, and until the artist showed it out. It then ran along a ditch under his studio, tinkling and splashing its way to the horse-pond, and thus to the Stour. Its brick bed in the kitchen stays smooth from its passage, but I have never been able to work out its science. But I can sit where the first master of this house sat and space myself in his dwelling. Beyond it in time there would arise and stretch a palace of beams beyond his comprehension. Celtic monks sought water for company. It was something going on, which spoke, which accompanied the heart-beat. They hugged the shore-line. Prayer ran with it.

The hut would slyly take in what would have been non-usable land and use it. Eventually it would be a dwelling house with some seventy acres. Although these would lie in distant halves because a high tongue of good arable would reach through it. This belonged to Garnon's Manor. They were Normans. And so for generations my farmers had to walk miles to work, humping their implements, wearying their plough horses. Not that there was much cornland when you got there. About twenty acres, maybe. Mostly it was alder carrs and bottoms, sopping wet places. But also a field-cum-orchard and a gravel pit. Quite a useful bit of ground if you knew how to get something from it. Around the house there were about twenty acres of good arable and about the same number of 'lottens' or pastures. Presumably these lots were let to neighbours for grazing. There was a big thatched barn and wide yard, and from Tudor days a substantiality. But a lot of water. It designed whatever had to be done here.

The village may have taken its name from Widermund, the ford-keeper. The Stour ran shallow where he lived and I see him as a business-like St Christopher, getting folk from Suffolk into Essex without too great a splash. However, the children especially will have none of the Widermund tale, much preferring a St George and the Dragon story which comes from the Worm in Wormingford. When I told it to them in the school, how the Dragon from our mere demanded virgins for dinner until Sir William Waldegrave our squire lanced it, one boy said, 'He'd go hungry these days, sir!' A World War One window in the church shows a crocodile devouring a poor girl, her white legs hanging from its jaws. And a belated St George. But give me Widermund of the Ford, the crossing-keeper of our two counties. I knew a miller's son who was named after him. Maybe he was there when the Bottengoms' man roofed the spring.

Twinned dizzy ashes announce the farm. Joined at the bole, perfectly fronded, at least fifty feet in the air, they have shaken off – Jane Austen – all shameful connections. Like most of today's villagers, they have no notion of toil or myth. Their roots are

The garden in winter

not in Hades and their tops are not in Paradise, and both their traditional usefulness and their ancient mystery, they are glad to announce, are washed away in running water. Pollarding, coppicing, cart-shafts, poles, lovely firewood, trees of the world, do not mention such things in their hearing. The only people they have met in their thirty or so years talk of botany, art and literature. Or call dogs. Or who ramble past at weekends. They have modelled for watercolours, even oils, and they have grown so tall that they are no longer parish-bound and can take a universal view of existence. They edge what was once the farm's biggest and most challenging field, a dipping saucer of land called Shoals, watery-laden just when you needed to plough it, but set aside now for badgers, rabbits, weeds and the occasional deer, if you ever heard of such a thing. Most of the Bottengoms land was a second best and you had to know it to grow it. Shoals! When Tom Wolsey the Ipswich man came to grief, Shakespeare said, 'he had sounded all the depths and shoals of honour.'

Ashes seed when they feel like it and this pair are sparse providers where birds are concerned, being enwrapped in their own loveliness. They shiver in the wind and throw out boughs with a calculated aim, which is to be beautiful. 'Welcome home, useless farm-dweller', they say. 'You are one of us. When did you grow corn and turnips in this paddy-field? When did you cry when the harvest was a wash-out?' Gilbert White noted how some ash-trees bore loads of keys every year whilst others none at all. 'The prolific ones are naked and unsightly: those that are sterile abound in foliage and carry their verdure a long while and are pleasing objects.' Across the track from these pleasing objects stand the 1987 gale-wrecked oaks whose crippled limbs are beginning to fall at last, and whose monstrous defects made them grand and pitiable, though somehow worse because of the amazing loveliness of this double ash, winter and summer.

That enchanting tree-describer Will Cohu, in his *Out of the Woods*, quotes contrary opinions on the ash. 'The Reverend William Gilpin, Victorian champion of the picturesque, remarked that 'the ash never contracts the least disgusting formality' – meaning that it was regally arbitrary and romantic in its wild appearance. More recently, the late, great dendrologist, Alan Mitchell, took a different view: 'The common ash has somehow become a byword in country literature and among poets for grace and elegance although in my view it is an exceptionally coarse and dull tree.'... He liked a good, thick, straight trunk he could get his arms around, but the ash was 'much forked and graceless'. Steady on!

But Mitchell would have been thinking of the ash in my lower horse-pond, another double-dweller but terrible to behold. An ash country filled with ash lanes and ash pools, ash deserts and ash dwellings for multitudinous inhabitants, and with the ash goddess Yggdrassil lurking in its shapeless tree territory to frighten the wits out of anyone who pries too near. And with her dragon in waiting, of course, Wormingford being dragon-land. Only what I see far beyond the pond mud in which this immense ash is rooted is the depth of agricultural toil, that seasonal labour which ceased in my boyhood and which you have to be pretty old to have witnessed. It is now almost impossible to describe day in, day out, physical toil. What it was like to give all one's bodily strength to the same few acres, year in, year out? This lower ash saw the apparently everlastingness of it and then, impossible at the time to believe, the going for good of it. This when I was writing *Akenfield*, though with no realisation that such a thing could happen even then. Farming went up and down, and toilers with it. And now the four hundred or so acres of farmland are sown and cropped by half a dozen drivers, young men who sit and steer. Men with machines have conquered men as machines and a millennia of craft and art, celebration and belief has vanished in a decade or two, sunk from sight. Sunk below this lovely wonderful ash which feeds on them still. Nothing else in my two acres except the timber of the farmhouse and the timber of this mighty tree is able to express what happened here for century after century as the sun rose and until it set, human limbs and ash limbs twisting and darkening in turn. Neither were spared as a living resource. Axe and saw went to the living ash for what the farm needed and its mad shape was defined by amputations.

Visitors don't know what to make of this ash, and are floored by its ivy. By its dead branches sticking out here and there, by its proportions, which are unreasonable and beyond the help of Paul the tree-surgeon, whose advice, if I was foolish enough to solicit it, would, knowing him, be, 'Let it be'. Generations have let this ash be, and it shows. The last plough horses drank in its shade about three o'clock every afternoon, hurrying when it came into view. John Constable often walked past it, and probably sketched it. He had a passion for bark. Although this particular bark is a limited sight, breaking surface just here and there in the swarming growth, it is worth looking at. A tender silver-brown fixed to the trunk like filigree, appearing here and there as a kind of treat. Otherwise ivy has become a tree itself and it is worth a bet as to what supports which, the climber or the climbed. Blackened boughs are gently cupped in imploring gestures and end in a bundle of sticks. Hollows and pools are contained in them. They make an ash city, a kind of Nineveh for birds, beasts and insects, whose population statistics are

Bottengoms Farm photographed by the author

incalculable. But a rough and ready place, with mean leaves and creaks and groans. Not to be outdone the base of the ash is leaned on by hollies and elders. These massed plants shove themselves against the north wind and help to keep me cosy. All the pruning is done by gales. Now and then pairs of magpies drive snowily from a particular bough like Olympic youths, white and perfect, to seize crusts. It is astonishing that these gleaming creatures can still almost instantaneously arouse blood lust in a countryman, a longing to kill them. We know why. But it is no longer justifiable, I try to explain. Not murder now and then? What a spoilsport. The magpies land with a bounce and chak-chak-chak-chak off in a music of sorts. The ash itself is a virtual tree orchestra of wood in senescence, some screams included, for it is frightening to die. I have woken up to find it hung with starlings. Visitors are apt to view it with alarm. Might a lump of it fall on me? Very likely. But I am unable to explain to them that I have appointed this ancient ash Memory Bank for Farm Labour because alone of all the still living witnesses to the purpose of Bottengoms it seems to have in its writhing roots and broken tips a notion of what it was like to let fields take all your strength.

Thus says the old ash, 'Follow your deeds as I talk.' These go as far as the farmyard wall where I am concerned. After this acres and acres of cornfields and grazing lots spread to the Chase, ending in a pair of double-dwellers' gardens turned thickets, the buildings vanished. And there is a tiny wedge of land called Malting Bottom, and everywhere flint in great quantities which the crop shoots appear to be able to push aside in order to keep their line. We are making a slow descent into the Stour valley here. Other yeoman's houses, neighbours of a millennium, are sprinkled through it, each in the old terms with just sufficient land to give independency. No more. It was along this faint track that 'our' horses made for the stables, the pond, the children, and the labourers for their ceaseless toil for a few shillings a week, and along it that the young labourers ran away to the city, to the railways, to the army, to the empire. To the Western Front. And down which Scottish Farmers came to put their backs into a new life, one with no experience of English rural servitude. Seeing our huge thistles, one of them knew at once what good soil it was, and prospered.

My old neighbour Hugh Barrett, who had served a farm apprenticeship not far from here, wrote wondrously about the last farm horses. Tears would fill his eyes should he happen to see jumps on television. Horses should not be asked to do such feats, their beloved bodies unnaturally spread, their fearful gaze ahead, their nearness to the knacker's yard. He would turn away. He would remember the farm horses of his – and my – boyhood. I include his description of what happened most working days here because it is the best farewell to a vanished agriculture I know.

'It was no good asking the Guv'nor what was sched-uled for the days work ahead at this time. He wouldn't say. At ten to six we finished the second cup and the second rock bun, tapped the barometer, and went out across the yard to the stable where for an hour or more George the head horseman (ploughman) had been at work feeding and grooming, and the under-horsemen were ready to harness up. The Guv'nor and George had a quiet word or two together while the rest of us stood waiting on them and their decisions, and the horses blew out the last grains of oats from the more abundant chaff in the mangers. Then, having organized everything to their liking, the Guv'nor would disappear towards the barn where the daymen would get their orders from him, and George relay ours. He began with his second in command, his brother Willy – and went down in hierarchical importance to third, fourth and fifth horsemen, telling each one what he was to do and the order in which the jobs must be done. A load of hay from the stackyard into the horse-yard; mangolds for the cowshed; a pair of horses to be shod by the village blacksmith (this was a job for me); two pairs to plough; a pair for the beet-lifting, and two in tumbrils for beet-carting. George never made a mistake: he, or he and the Guv'nor between them, could reckon up to the minute how long each job should take, making automatic adjustments for the different men and different horses ...

The Home stable had ties for fourteen horses and when I was there it was full of pure-bred Suffolks with traditional Suffolk names. George's pair were Blossom, the smallest mare in the stable and the most willing puller I've ever met with, and Bowler, a gelding with unusually good feet. He was a favourite for beet-hoeing because he never walked on the rows. Willy's pair were mixed too: a tall gelding called Captain and a biggish mare, Matchett, with an almost flaxen mane and tail. Third horseman Walter had Diamond, with a star on her nose, and Duke, a gaunt animal of great size and reputed to be twenty years old. Then there were two Boxers – Big Boxer and Little Boxer-Major, Kitty, Gypsy, and Ginger – a mountain of a horse who, as the men said, 'came off the streets' and was inclined to be mangy. Ginger had pulled a coal cart at the docks, and was good in traffic but hopeless in any job like horse-hoeing, because he floundered all over the place and put his ugly great feet on the seedlings. He was usually left for the odd jobs round the yards and was everybody's unfavourite.

Nowadays the stable is empty. Matchett survived until 1959, I think – I saw her last about then, standing alone and forlorn in a corner of Horse Meadow, flaxen tail to the wind, her head hanging, her lower lip drooping, her ribs and hip bones visible beneath the skin: a sad

The manger at Bottengoms photographed by Charles Hall

picture, as though she had forgotten the time when the meadow was alive with good companions, and didn't want to remember.

But in the thirties the stables were the centre, the powerhouse of the farm. I suppose there were seven or eight hundred acres of arable land, and most of it had to be ploughed, harrowed, drilled, rolled and harvested with horse-drawn implements every year. The one tractor – an International 10/20 – was used for heavy cultivating and neither the tractor nor its driver were thought much of by the horse people.'

Hugh awed me in another way because just before his farm apprenticeship he had taken part in Flaherty's classic film *Man of Aran*. I wish now I had asked him how this came about – a sixteen-year-old from Colchester becoming an actor in a kelp economy. I would have been his age when I saw this black-and-white masterpiece with its bleak women and seaweed fields. He was farming near me at Great Glemham in Suffolk when we met, his house full of beautiful children and his brother Roderic's paintings. Small fields such as you get in east Suffolk. My horse-pond and its sentinel ash brought back Hugh's voice, its radical intelligence and passion. Bottengoms Farm would, I suppose, have had a pair of work horses and a horseman for its forty acres of arable, plus a pony for the trap. This was where they drank century after century, sinking belly-high in the blissful coolness in July, throwing up their huge heads in the shade, and the water running ceaselessly, clouding then clearing. For ever and ever. I have waded naked in it to weed it and rake its outlets, and it became a liquid silk on my skin. Dead ash had to be dragged from it, soddenly preserved boughs looking like spars from the *Mary Rose*. In the spring its surface is a mat of marsh marigold, *caltha palustris*, and in late summer a diadem of dragonflies. But there are weeks when it can descend into sullenness like a Thomas Hardy place for suicide.

To reach the river I pass the old Bottengoms fields on the left. They heave themselves skywards. Oxen would have dragged wooden ploughs over them as late as the eighteenth century. The ploughman would have had to hold down the plough with all his might to do more than scrape the surface. An ox is a meditative beast and turning the winter soil was snail-going. East and north winds would whip around, and the shoals would glitter. Though few of those here with its steep runaway. Sarsen stones would be encountered and carried to the hedge. Flints would fly away from the wooden ploughshare in splinters. 'Loving land' – clinging clay – would build up on the ploughman's boots until he could barely walk. Rain would go through his clothes to his skin. But the sun would shine and both he and the oxen would be turned to joy. Who he was no one will ever know, he and all his predecessors and successors, the men who made all the fields. And to a good tune in summer.

'Much rural music was born of boredom', wrote Dorothy Hartley:

> 'Continuous repetitive movement induces rhythm … the gifted musician was always a rare person, and would probably evade field work and be well rewarded for his skill … We – I – try to imagine the music of the landworker when he herded his beasts on the common or worked in penfold or field. With long hours, often working alone, he would have plenty of time to practise, and he would hear and incorporate the sounds around him.

Bottengoms Farm photographed by English Heritage

Many made their own instruments, usually woodwind, for strings are better under cover, as wind and rain affect the gut. The wooden pipes in common use were of all manner of forms: ...Most rural music was pipe music and song.'

John Clare, ploughing, claimed his 'right to song'. David in his state-of-the-art cab, high up like an Indian prince on his elephant, is plugged into his favourite group as he ploughs one of my fields in an afternoon. Pitch is never his problem. This could still be company.

At first the yeomen asked for bread alone of their fields, then the famous Norfolk four-course menu of crops and rests, Fallow, Barley, Clover, Wheat. Or Fallow, Barley, Pease, Wheat, or any variation so long as the soil did nothing for a year. Then turnips arrived for the sheep on the lottens, and things were different. Some farmers even grew grasses in the rotation, although they would have been mad to do so at Bottengoms, although it was a little farm which was made up half and half with crops and stock. All those horses, cows, chickens, goats, pigs, sheep, and now only my white cat to lounge around the place, and the wild creatures to animate it. And all those women and girls, and boys and men, and all those children out to work at eight. And all that love and hate, sex and dying, and most of all, that relentless toil. And none of these things leaving what one might call an identifiable mark. Just husks.

John Clare wrote,

'Old Shepherd Newman dyd this Morning an old tenant of the fields & the last of the old shepherds of the fields are now left desolate & and his old haunts look like houses disinhabited the fading woods seem mourning in the autumn wind how often hath he seen the blue skye the green fields & woods & and the seasons changes & now he sleeps unconsious of all what a desolate mystery doth it leave round the living mind.'

Sir Cedric Morris photographed by RB

SURVIVAL

OLD FARMS SANK OR SWAM IN THE TWENTIETH CENTURY. Tottered, fell into ruin, were no more. Farmers fled from them. Owls and tramps took them over. Suicides drowned in their water-butts. Ploughs rusted in their barns. But their orchards fruited and their wells continued to be fed with springs. What pulled them down was the penury of their fields, the unmanageable acres, the mad hedges, the accusation of good soil left unattended. An abandoned ship or factory or mine is bad enough, but a given-up farm contains an element of sacrilege which makes it doubly unwanted both economically and spiritually. Those who did not farm before the Great War and who could not understand this, wrote to the newspapers and spoke from the pulpit about 'the flight from the land'.

Bottengoms Farm did not so much fall-in as fall into abeyance. Took a deep breath and began the waiting game. Its ruin was small enough not to threaten the scenery. It could sink back into the soil without leaving a tragic mark. Or artists and such rural oddities, or gypsies even, people without land values, might perch in it without danger of depression. There were little wildernesses like it all over East Anglia where bikes were propped in the sheds, the washing hung out and the fire blazed for a few bob a week. And whose tenants' hearts did not break when wild flowers conquered the corn.

In the 1880s, when seven years' rain and the North American grain ships, between them, destroyed British agriculture, and the squire's daughter received the yeoman's farm as part of her dowry, it was hardly worth the cultivating. Forty years later her executors conveyed it to Harry Munson, a farmer in the next village, for the sum of £1820, and he after the harvest of 1936 to Herbert Lewis of the neighbouring Maltings Farm for £1200, and he to Captain John Nash, Official War Artist, in 1944 for £700. That is the buildings only, the fifty or so acres which remained of the original farm being absorbed in the surrounding cultivation. Thus ended a yeoman's lot. John Nash was not less than exultant. Two horse ponds – 'Never pass up a good pond' – two acres or so of every kind of soil a gardener could lust after and buildings galore. As for the trees, the elms and ashes, the tremendous oaks and the banks begging a nut-walk, and the paddock asking for an orchard, they took his breath away. Only when a farm becomes calamitous can it become something other.

Never again would it be 'All that freehold farm with the messuage or farm house outbuildings closes pieces or parcels of land belonging thereto called "Bottingoms" otherwise "Botten-hams"' (and now Bottengoms), a name out of Mervyn Peake and doomed to be everlastingly spelled out on the telephone. Never more would its arable, pasture, yards etc. be coloured yellow for buyer after short-term buyer. It would be a Dwelling House.

John and Christine Nash, Wormingford, 1930

Down to the Dwelling House

Steps from the B-road to the unlettered track
Return me daily to my Dwelling House,
As the deeds proclaim it.
Carts, herds and farming feet have impacted this flint mile.
Grass the height of axeltrees has spared its crown.

I tread the grass to subdue this crown,
To stay it from doing more than it does,
Which is to stroke the bellies of cars.
My slight levelling might just save
A slicing of their exhaustive parts.

Intending guests telephone to ask,
Not, 'How are you?' but 'How is the track?'
All over England comes the question,
'How is your track?' It is most enquired of.
I consider then its metal, its middle rising proud,
And answer, 'Fine'. And indeed it is, most fine,
Most serviceable for its early intention,
Which was to carry farming feet, carts
And herds down to the Dwelling House.

But how is the track for Saabs and Minis,
Fiats even? This is what my guests are asking,
Though too polite to be that explicit.
I hear them rumbling away with low clearance
And self concern. Is it possible they might
Walk an uninitialled mile
From a B-road to a Dwelling House?

Take today, the Annunciation,
I tread the crown whilst fetching milk,
Ever thoughtful of these riders.
I see the cold stream pastures shining,
The corn hill pressing against the sky,
The March plants making cushions,
Black medick, agrimony, chervil, nettle,
Of course, all the new unravelling leaf.
Flower and wheat on the move.
I hear the wind answering the wires, feel

The track thinking back to what farming feet
Asked of it. Rough walkers on rough ground
Who trod it without assurances.

The old byre at Bottengoms photographed by Charles Hall

THE SEE-SAW OF EXISTENCE

OLD PAPERS FLUTTER ABOUT IN OLD FARMS. TWO AT
Bottengoms eloquently betray its ups and downs. The house
was new when the famous East Anglian wool trade collapsed after
centuries of prosperity. The glorious architecture it left in its
wake rises above the combined fields, the commuter routes and
the brilliant landscape. But in the early seventeenth century a
combination of circumstances drew a line under its seemingly
bottomless wealth. The clothiers, as they were called, fled the
scene, abandoning their peerless churches and wooden mansions
for Massachusetts, Ireland and the Cotswolds. The disaster was
great. A medieval economy fell. For those who stayed at home,
and these included the farmers and weavers of the Stour Valley,
it was starvation. Hanging on the wall is this cry of despair.

The Clothiers' Petition to His Majestie With His Majestie's Gracious Answer.
The humble Petition of the Clothiers of Suffolk, and the Townes of Dedham
and Langham in Essex.

May it please Your Majestie

The pressing fears that hath befallen your loving
Subjects, especially those of the City of London, in whom

the breath of our Trade and livelihood consisteth, have so blasted their hopes, that the Merchants forbear exportation: our cloth for the most part, for the space of this 18 months remain upon our hands, our stocks lying dead therein, and we can maintain our trade no longer. The cries for food of many thousands of the poor, who depend on this Trade, do continually press us, not without threats, and some beginnings of mutinies, so that, if some speedy relief do not intervene, we can expect no less than confusion.

For help hereof your supplicants have petitioned both Houses of Parliament, and well knowing that the life of all supply next under God, resteth in Your Royal Self... we are emboldened in all humility to petition Your Majesty to let one word fall from Your Majesty to Your Parliament in our behalfe...

Charles I was getting out of his coach at Greenwich when this was handed to him. He asked these River Stour men to attend him in the Presence Chamber. He gave his answer in the garden. He said that they were right to tell him these things and that 'he would take further care of it'. But the Civil War and the random nature of market forces, as disastrous to ordinary folk as they are now, entirely altered the conditions in which the yeomanry reconstructed their farmhouses. A profound religious attitude took hold. It was known as the Godly People of the Stour Valley and stretched many miles on either side of the river. There was a second wave of iconoclasm led by a Suffolk farmer named William Dowsing, this time against the idolatry in church windows. Dowsing kept a diary of his smashings. It makes grim reading. Often parishes were too poor to replace the painted glass with clear glass, and wild weather tore into the churches, making them unusable. Godly People stayed at home in ceaseless prayer.

In the 1630s, a local lawyer named John Winthrop, grandson of a rich Lavenham clothier, sought a new England. Ship-loads of East Anglians followed him to Massachusetts, where he founded Boston. They took their seed corn with them and all the Suffolk and Essex flowers came up with it. Their descendants haunt our countryside as they comb it for ancestors. They also take down the old plain glass in the churches and replace it with ancestral pictures, heraldry and pride. They bear our names, writing them in the registers of the Band B farmhouses. They tap on the door of Bottengoms and send Christmas cards, and are a New England aristocracy. In Boston they took me up a tall building and pointed to a kind of smudge by the Charles River. 'The stockade was about there.' It would have been like going to the moon. They sent home for nails and hinges. Did my yeoman go with them, lurching up the track in his wagon, looking back, staring forward? I still can't quite understand why it took so many weeks to sail the Atlantic. Is there a New Bottengoms? How could there be? Would it not be an oxymoron'?

Other than the deeds, the most telling document which goes with the farmhouse is a much-thumbed edition of John Cullyer's inestimable *Gentleman's and Farmer's Assistant*, 1798. Two and sixpence. Land was measured in acres, rods and perches, which made it exceedingly difficult to assess if for example you were selling a growing crop of clover. Cullyer's solution was to change these measurements into yards. Everything on a Georgian farm was reduced to yards, or a man's step. His tables remind me of bellringers' changes. Mr Runnacles owned this indispensable square volume. It shows every sign of having been carried round the fields. Richard Girling gave it to me when he heard I had inherited Bottengoms and one could say that it had come home. What it most reminds me of is the mysterious way which those who could barely read and write had with figures.

The little house in which I was born was thatched. Here is *A Table for Measuring Thatcher's work from One to Sixty-four Feet long, and from One to Twenty-five Feet High. Or a Stack.*

> Measure the length of it in Feet, and also the
> Slant height, from the Eaves to the Top, then
> in the Tables, under the Length of the House
> or Stack in the top Column, and opposite to
> the Height of the Roof in the left hand Column
> you have the content of one Side in Yards and
> Square Feet, and if the Dimensions be the same
> on both Sides, double the Content of one Side
> gives the Content of both Sides.

Easy, you see. Nothing to it. Two youthful thatchers have been talking to me, computers at the ready. They have plenty of work, they say, reed or straw. Do they cut their sign – like the old thatchers? They shake their heads and smile. 'Suppose a Stack is 17 feet from the Eaves to the Top, and 94 Feet round at the Eaves, half the Circumference is 47 Feet …' But I don't try this on. They regard me shyly. 'Yes, plenty of work'. They come from East Bergholt, where John Constable lived.

John Nash, 1967

FLOORS

CEILINGS AND WALLS ARE RARELY TOUCHED, FLOORS AND latches have been intimately touched every day for centuries. Here they show the touching. Other than the polished boards in the Victorianised parlour, the entire ground floor is bricked. Herring-bone pattern in what was the Elizabethan kitchen, English-bond everywhere else. Both wood and brick floors were a sensational advance on the mud floors which were laid down when the farmhouse was built, and people were very proud of them. The poet George Crabbe, courting Miss Elmy, heard her mother shouting at a new servant, 'What, the likes of you scrub bricks like these!' And he watched her fall on her knees in a baptising that was worthy of them. Cottage 'restorers' in the fifties pulled them up and threw them out. It was the first thing they did. The second was to lay concrete for the fitted carpet. It was from then on that, for the first time, the timeless intimacy between flesh and floor ceased.

Now and then, in a Mrs Elmy mood, I scrub a brick floor. It comes up a primrose white and sometimes the grasses on which the bricks were set to dry appear on the wet surface, and reveal a ghostly Georgian sunshine. The bricks are thin and heavy. Some sit tight, others have shifted and have become musical, giving out elfin zylophonic notes when they are trodden. 'You want to get them bricks fixed'. But I like brick music. I first listened to it in a Suffolk brickfield as the men, their hands bandaged in leather strips, loaded new bricks onto barrows. The most favoured were Suffolk Whites. They chimed all the way to the building site. Now and then I feel them shifting under a rug like living things, this time soundlessly. I should get them fixed. But there comes a moment in life when mending stops. When I brought some house failure to its previous owner, his answer was always the same. 'It will see me out.' This is what the farmhouse did for five hundred years, see its owners out.

For much longer than this almost every dwelling, palaces even, had mud floors. Here is Mr Robert Edmunds' recipe for a mud floor. He is quoting the seventeenth-century Henry Best. How to lay a mud floor. The earth was to be dug and raked until the moulds were 'indifferent small'. The water was to be brought in 'seas' and in 'great tubs or hoggsheads or sleddes'. The earth was then to be watered until it was a 'soft puddle'. It was then allowed to lie a fortnight until the water had settled and the material had begun to grow hard again. Then the floor was to be 'melled' and beaten down with wooden paddles to a smooth finish. The generally used mud floors were porous, and so absorbed 'any wet matter, particularly that of nitrous content; for no one was fastidious about sanitation... Mud floors were very dusty and difficult to keep clean. In dry weather they were often strewn with rushes and damp plants. Some of the better-class houses had mud for the floor mixed with a proportion of bullock's blood, fine clay and bone chips, which dried hard and gave it the appearance of black marble when polished ... The use of sand and lime as flooring for cottages was new to most areas until well into the eighteenth century.'

My Flemish bond floors are hard set in their ways. Some are locked together with barely a knife blade between them. Others lie an inch apart in black ditches along which the copper-water has flown in soapy gulleys. Until John Nash came to the house in World War Two the actual stream which had fed Bottengoms ever since it was built ran across the great kitchen, in via the larder, out by the front door, so that one never need to go outside for domestic water. This is where the washing copper and the brewing copper stood, the massive stone sink and the bread oven. So the dips in the brickwork were not only the evidence of the sacred rite of scrubbing. This low room was a delta land through whose crevasses and scrubbed-out dips water of one kind or another poured, trickled, hung around or sped. It was scrubbed with a broom. Countless washdays have left the copper-stand bricks rounded and edgeless. The big stone sink in which the children stood to be flannelled with a heavy hand, rinsed and lifted down, does duty in the garden. But the door where the men pulled off their 'loving-land', i.e. soil-clinging boots, still retains its bar or oak, a lump of wood which when slotted through iron bands at bedtime, out-defended any key.

Feet are so delicate. The tiniest bush (prickle) will lame them. With only an oblong of rag rug by the hearth, with boots drying in the corner, with shoes for best, naked or barely covered feet made their way daily over my bricks for ages. The white feet of girls, the brown feet of boys, the crippled feet of the old. The 'dead feet' which Thomas Hardy still saw walking in. No other part of an ancient house has so experienced the bodies of those who lived in it. Foot-worn entrances, hand-worn scrubbings. And three sprawling bedchambers with wide elm-board floors. Coffin wood.

Wood which stays dry, even in the grave. And the master-and-his-wife room, running down hill, the elm boards patched with blocks where the rats have entered. There for reign after reign the country couples tossed, copulated, slept, talked, worried, suffered, died. 'What a lovely guest-room!' the visitors cry. It is the same room and the same bed in which I slept as a boy, feet in the air. In which Paul Nash slept. There was a drawing of his elms. And a heavy little board oil of sheep by John. And a randy tile by the washbasin of 'The Sailor's Return'. And a lamp-blackened ceiling, and rickety 'good' furniture, a full-length swing looking-glass for narcissists and a whiff of historic occupancy.

The hugger-muggerness of life in a farmhouse before there could be such an outlandish thing as a room of one's own required one to see without looking and to hear without listening. And certainly to speak innocently. Single labourers mounted

Wild Garden, Winter by John Nash, 1959

the ladder to the attic, there to freeze or bake. A maid-servant or two would find rest in a screened corner. There was little or no light other than that from the sun, the moon and the stars. The dogs and cats did best before the cinders. And all those white and brown, clean and dirty, perfect and imperfect feet running to and fro over the bare floors.

It was, without stop,
The time of the seasons and the constellations
The time of milking and the time of harvest
The time of the coupling of man and woman
And that of beasts. Feet rising and falling.
Eating and drinking. Dung and death.
Here in this house, all the time.

MATRIMONY DURING THE BUILDING OF THE HOUSE

WHO CAME HERE? WHO HELPED HERE? WHOSE HANDS raised the new beams, and the old beams from the dust? Since no one will ever know when the first – or third – Bottengoms was pulled down, or most likely fell down, and who helped to raise it during Elizabeth's time, I thought that I might get a glimpse of these useful neighbours by reading the Marriage Register in the church. And here I became intoxicated by their lovely names.

The first couple to process from 'the body of the church' to 'the Lord's Table', the parson singing or saying, 'Thy wife shall be as the fruitful vine upon the walls of thine house, thy children like the olive branches round about thy house', were William Lufte and Margret Armidyll. Or perhaps he was William Luste, f's being not what they are now. It was the first yeare of our Sovereign Lady Queen Elizabeth – 1558. And it was mid-summer. So the hay-making was done and there was a space until harvest. There was one ring and it was on her finger. Had he 'tried' her? Most young husbands had tried their girls to make sure that there would be children, or had 'got caught' – i.e. been obliged to marry the girl who had become pregnant. Thus I see a procession of some sixty brides and grooms winding from the church to the barns, their ears full of words from the Edwardian Prayer Book and lute music, their persons trailing eglantine. The Wife could be a 'minor', as could the Husband. It was all right as long as it was put in the book. Here is the procession of their names. They walk from the parish church in chronological order until James I rides down from Scotland.

Umphrey Rysbey and Joane Clarke
Alexander Sturdyfall and Annis Bird
Harry Lay and Ide Gaunt
William Seaburrowe and Annis Ewers
George Knops and Thomazin Myller
Henry Hoye and Margery Profitt
Robert Hilles and Margaret Mayston
Thomas Coo and Anes Hollburrowes
John Chardy and Margret Creake
Roberte Lessingwell and Joan Pamitt
William Dex and Jane Rimakers
William Petycan and Elizabeth Allin
Thomas Higham, esq., and Marye Nudigate
Leonarde Hartlife and Joane Lurkine

They were on my fields, down my track, in my rooms. Giving a hand.

'Where the dead feet walked in'

THE PROGRESS

IT IS AUGUST AGAIN. THEY ARE HARVESTING ONCE MORE. I am standing on Lodge Hill looking down into Smallbridge, for the once great house which is still impressive though a shadow of its original self, lies beneath me, vulnerable and exposed. It is on the opposite bank of the Stour, thus in Suffolk. The Lodge of Lodge Hill is being excavated by the archaeologists every Tuesday. It is hot and cool by turn as the breeze comes and goes. The firs on Christmas-tree Hill stir. Rabbits do a bunk. In a haze I can see high ground where Edmund was crowned King of the East Angles. Dust from the combine is suffocating like the desert dust in *Lawrence of Arabia* when the hero makes his galloping entry. The young man in the cab waves.

August in London in 1561, the heat, the disease. Why not go to Wormingford? Why not put a few miles between Elizabeth and Robert? She is twenty-eight and he has conveniently lost his wife Amy, who fell downstairs and broke her neck. This the year before. Oh the boon of the Home Counties. There vast new brick houses await their baptism of royalty. And so the Queen arrives just below me, the miles-long sausage of her baggage-train squeezing through the wool lanes, and all flags flying. Her host

The Barn, Wormingford by John Nash R.A.

William Waldegrave is twenty-two. His maternal grandmother was cousin to the Queen's mother and also to her successors Queens Katherine Howard and Jane Seymour. Or so they say. William has built an enormous house with forty-four hearths and re-modelled a deer-park along the river, only finishing Smallbridge weeks before the Progress comes into view. It has taken Elizabeth ten days (forty-five minutes in the car) to come from Ipswich. But then she has called at Shelley which even now is a hold-up, being so delightful.

House-building is infectious. The Listed Buildings man from Cambridge thought that Bottengoms Farm would have been re-constructed in the sixteenth century, the yeoman-owner prudently re-using the wood. But I must consult Leigh about this.

Leigh knows more about beams than anyone else in the world. All the same, what with Sir William's demand for timber and that of the valley farmers, one senses that Elizabeth travelled through a far less treed landscape than the one in which I live. And I should add, the one I came to when the elms died and Duncan my farmer neighbour gave me twenty-five broad-leafed trees to fill the grim gap, and which are now sky-high.

Elizabeth I approaches. She is by all accounts no beauty though wonderful to behold. She enters Smallbridge grounds in her coach and is followed by the twenty coaches of her ladies and women. Goodness knows how many gentlemen and men ride and run around her. There are sweet trumpets.

Elizabeth is young and tall with red hair and an oblong face, fine eyes and an athletic frame which walking and dancing would preserve until her dying day. The loglike effigy on his tomb would not have done justice to her host, so in his twenties, and his best clothes, and bowing to his new floorboards, I can reckon him a charmer.

It is this very year, 1561, that the Queen of France was widowed and returned to her kingdom of Scotland. Mary was eighteen. And at this moment Titian painted his *Diana and Acteum* and his *Diana and Callisto*, two pictures which might at a stretch allegorise the Queen watching the stags being slaughtered at Smallbridge, seeing them driven towards her royal box by hounds and disemboweled on the summer grass. For Actaeon was a young huntsman who, for having caught Diana taking a bathe, was torn to pieces by her dogs, then changed into a stag so that he could always be hunted down. Diana was like many a woman who abjured marriage and preferred a life with her maidens, the bent bow and the quiver, and her ferocious hounds. Their 'music' arrives in my winter wood when the North Essex and West

Suffolk Hunt passes this way. Pale graffiti of antlers is scratched on the columns in church. Also a message in a Tudor hand, which I can't quite make out. Diana's flowers are the poppy and the dittany (Dittander) *Lepidium latifolium*, the latter a hot-rooted flower which became a leprosy herb. Llewelyn Powys called one of his heroines Dittany. Titian's second painting, *Diana and Callisto*, its surface hardly dry when Elizabeth descended on Smallbridge, is of one of Diana's attendants who had an affair with Jupiter and whose pregnancy was discovered when she bathed, and who was turned into a bear for her presumption, and the bear turned into a constellation to save her from being hunted.

Elizabeth, Queen-goddess of the English, brought her portable bed when she Progressed. Sir Roy Strong describes it. Was Robert ever in it? That was the question which no one dared to ask. One senses not. No turning him into a king. Elizabeth would sleep above a pile of her ladies. And just down there. And for two nights only. And hearing what I often hear at Bottengoms, Thomas Vautor's 'Sweet Suffolk Owl' – 'With feathers like a lady bright'. And lying in that bed and smelling of marjoram. A later portable bed, the one she used for travelling to her various palaces, had 'hangings of cloth and silver trimmed with gold and silver lace and fringe'. Together with the white satin ceiling to the tester they were painted with three hundred and forty-seven sprigs of flowers. The bed was of walnut, ornate with the Queen's Beasts in gilt and colour, 'while above nodded six huge bunches of multi-coloured ostrich plumes spangled with gold.'

Here is the bill for Smallbridge, 11–14 August, 1561, in pounds, shillings and pence:

12 August 1561

Dispenses (Steward's Room)	£7 . . 10 . . 8	
Buttil Buttilia (Buttery)	19 . . 0 . . 0	
Gard (Garden stuff)	7 . . 10 . . 2	and three farthings
Coquina (Cook's Room)	28 . . 14 . . 0	
Pullia (Poultry)	16 . . 19 . . 8	
Scutt (Dishes etc.)	7 . . 0 . . 0	
Salsar (Salted meat)	1 . . 0 . . 8	
Aula (Servants' Hall)	1 . . 3 . . 0	
Stabulum (Stables)	25 . . 8 . . 6	halfpenny
Vadia (Wages)	10 . . 0 . . 0	
Elimosina (Alms)	6 . . 0 . . 0	
Total:	£130 . . 6 . . 9	farthing

13 August 1561

Dispenses	7 . . 10 . . 8	
Buttil	18 . . 5 . . 5	
Gard	7 . . 16 . . 11	farthing
Coquina	29 . . 17 . . 10	
Pullia	16 . . 7 . . 2	
Scutt	5 . . 19 . . 4	
Salsar	19 . . 4	
Aula	4 . . 9 . . 6	
Stabulum	19 . . 11 . . 6	halfpenny
Vadia	10 . . 0 . . 0	
Elimosima	4 . . 0	

Total: Thousands of pounds in today's money.

Here is my hand,
My dear lover England,
I am thine both with mind and heart,
For ever to endure,
Thou mayest be sure,
Until death us two do part.

Miles of onions for the supermarket now line her route. But deer occasionally are seen, groups of very still creatures before they bound off to Arger Fen and Tiger Hill. Gliders tilt overhead. The bells they may have heard during the Progress are rung on Sundays, though in changes, which would have puzzled them. The meres from which they fetched their fish and duck glitter like her jewels, and are full of legends. Combine dust will blot both out for a while. History goes over and over the same ground, treading it down, pushing it up, scratching its claims.

My friend Andrew White and his fellow archaeologists have been digging up Elizabeth's 'standing' or royal box for viewing the hunt. The site was betrayed by the hill being called Lodge Hill and a ferret hole. Andrew says the organisation for such a hunt meant that at first the deer were kept in parks and fed on hay to maintain stocking levels. Within the deer park a system of paddocks and fences – 'Parokes' – were used to control the movement of the animals so that the huntsmen could be ensured of a sizeable bag. 'Toils' – temporary nets and fences – were then used to herd the deer. 'Standings' – raised platforms or towers, ours at Wormingford was a tower – were then built on an elevated vantage point. These buildings might vary from a simple wooden open structure to a four-storey lodge, or a hunting tower with a view from the roof.

A royal hunt in the Queen's father's time would have seen

John Nash and Jock Cranbrook fishing for pike in the Stour, 1958, photographed by Kurt Hutten,

wave after wave of deer meeting showers of crossbow bolts, with large greyhounds dragging down those not killed outright. Carts would trundle backwards and forwards at intervals to pick up the slain animals and take them to be laid out for Henry to survey them at the conclusion of the sport. His daughter's hunts were less bloodthirsty affairs. She would be content with a bag of maybe 10 to 15 deer shot with her own bow. At the beginning of the hunt the Queen might be invited to view the 'droppings' of the first animal to be hunted so that she could assess its condition and show off her knowledge. At the end of the day all the dead deer would be laid out in a row below her Standing and the huntsmen would gather round to blow the 'Mort' to signal the deaths. After which Elizabeth would inspect the carcasses, be handed a sharp knife, and slit open the throat of the fattest buck to demonstrate that it was 'high Grease'. Then supper and dancing. She with her boy host. Then on to the not so youthful Earl of Oxford at Hedingham, whose son would be a verbose poet who some people claim to be William Shakespeare. Chance would be a fine thing.

The World War Two poet Keith Douglas, surveying his comrades in the Western Desert, wrote:

These plains were their cricket pitch
and in the mountains the tremendous drop fences
brought down some of the runners. Here then
under the stones and earth they dispose themselves,
I think with their famous unconcern.
It is not gunfire I hear, but a hunting horn.

THE DWINDLING

BAR THE HOUSE AND ITS YARDS, ALL THE LAND HAD pretty much filtered away by the winter of 1944. John Nash had painted its fields and meadows from 1929 on, and had met its various short-term residents, the lively Smith boys and a tubercular army officer spending his last days in a bell-tent, and the occasional vagrant in the barn. Being an official war artist the second time had not gelled. Docks and bollards instead of Flanders, and being middle aged. 'My heart wasn't in it', he said, not as it had been when, frightened, shaking and brilliant, he had recorded *Over the Top*. What now preoccupied him was the making of a garden. He owned – the signed and sealed possession of it – an amalgam of soils more various than seemed possible in one small spot. As the war dragged to a close his impatience to dig and plant them took precedence in his head over art, not to mention the repair of the house. The latter stares across the river into his friend Adrian Bell's 'Creems', a yeoman's dwelling so tumbledown when the writer found it that his mother thought he should put a match to it. John and Adrian had collaborated on a book called *Men and the Fields* just before the war whose text and lithographs paid a kind of last homage to the scenes which the final yeomen had created in the stretch of valley between them, the artist at that moment mourning the loss of his little son William, killed in a motor accident. *Men and the Fields* has an unconscious 'requiescat' quality about it which the future scientific farming of the area would destroy. Not to mention the glamorisation of its poor old properties, one or two with aeroplanes in their sheds.

When Captain Nash signed the deeds of Bottengoms Farm in 1944 he had bought himself some dense nightingale cover and a rat-run. You needed a rip to get to the front door. None of this was thought odd at the time. Country people slashed their way about; the July flowers met over country children's heads. After John had written the cheque, a pair of builders from Nayland moved in. War-time regulations only allowing a few bobsworth of materials, whatever else was needed was found among the plentiful dereliction which lay around. It was his wife, the artist Christine Kühlenthal, who made Bottengoms more than just habitable – who recreated its spirit, nothing less. She swept it out, ran-up curtains on her Singer, scrubbed its bricks, lit its grates, imported fine cats, and painted precious old things such as its Georgian corner-cupboard 'stone' and Charleston-rose. She admired the way an occasional leaf would deck the bathwater and encouraged bindweed to climb the saucepan-stand. At Bottengoms one was never entirely outside or inside, and later on chain-smoking, paraffin, Winsor and Newton paints, damp, Ronuk, seeds, cooking, classy soaps, old uniforms and fishing gear, the village theatrical society's wardrobe, lights (for the cats) and preserves in the cold larder would combine to give the house an odour which for a moment would take one back as one entered the front door. Its old dairy was filled with – coal. John's studio to the north was plaster-boarded, given a

Christine Kühlenthal (Nash), 1938

coke-stove and a rush mat from Christine's days at the Omega Workshop with her friend Dora Carrington, and the farmer's parlour was called the drawing-room, and thus it began, the life I found there when I arrived. The furniture which Carter Patterson had brought from Buckinghamshire, including the Steinway grand, soon buried beneath a thousand letters and scores. A horse and cart had carried this down. It was August and very hot. 'The horse died', explained John. A car battery started the pump if you were lucky. Paintings swung on nails. Books rocked on shelves. Pot plants and botanic specimens filled the windows. Should in summer the bathwater fail, John would seize a towel and jump in the pond. There was a great deal of music and much hard work. Old chaps and boys toiled outside. Eric Ravilious's widow contributed his greenhouse. Mountains of vegetables

Christine Nash by Ronald Blythe, 1970

Eric Ravilious's greenhouse at Bottengoms, 1970

and fruit came in from the wilderness. I cleaned out the ponds. Jam and pickles boiled away. Ron from the village shop brought the order. Doors were never locked – no keys anyway. Visiting lovers creaked overhead. In the evenings I read aloud by lamplight, Henry James, L.P. Hartley. Hotwater bottles and a minute whisky. Cinders were raked before breakfast and spread on the paths. At ten we each painted, wrote or vanished. Years and years of this. There were no parties, or rather we went to other people's parties which John adored and Christine despised somewhat. 'Oh, darling, how good to be home again!' Their activities held an element of regret.

Ronald Blythe cleaning the pond, 1950

Paul Nash once came. It was 1946 – before my time. He was very ill, dying in fact. Gas from the Great War, plus asthma, was seeing him off. They told me about it. He had stayed the night, sleeping in the great sloping chamber with his feet in the air, as I would do until I inherited the house, for John and Christine did not take kindly to suggestions, such as a couple of bricks under the bedhead. This was the room in which centuries of yeomen had slept. It was a birth, marriage and death room.

It had a humpy ceiling and a tiny basket grate and all Paul and John's illustrated books, photograph albums and World War One poets. It was hard to sleep. A single sheepskin lay on

Paul and Bunty Nash

John and Paul Nash at Tite Street, London, photographed by Lance
Sieveking, 1935

the splintery floor. Jack Frost drew pictures on the panes at
Christmas. Christine brought tea in at eight, sat on the bed and
told tales out of school. What an awakening for a young writer.
Was I warm enough?

When he arrived Paul had only quite recently painted the
Battle of Britain. Its mordant pendant had been *Totes Meer*, a
Luftwaffe scrapheap. The Air Ministry had thought it excellent
propaganda, not comprehending. Now he himself was taking
off as he had dreamed of doing since boyhood. To fly is the
most common of dreams. But first he must see his brother
properly earthed, for was it not John's dream to be properly
planted? Glancing around the steep, patched-up old farmhouse,
its beams corseted with big iron stays from the blacksmith, the
north studio above the stackyard, he said, 'This is the place for
you!' Critics were always thinking that, being brothers, they had

to share their space. John's reply to this was to give Paul a drawing of machine-gunners holding off all comers from the top of the fearful old ash tree, all spikes and batons.

Paul had travelled by train from Oxford, and John had fetched him by car from Colchester station. Just before he set out he had written to his old friend the poet Gordon Bottomley,

'Well, I had no operation but I did have pneumonia with variations such as speechless flu, Endorma [oedema] & a small packet of dry pleurisy to top up with. It all began with the stalwart reliable guaranteed heart beginning to show signs of strain. Really. I'm a war victim, Gordon! I painted so many outsize pictures for the M of I [Ministry of Information] that the strain crocked up my heart which of course I suppose had been already coughed into a slight decline by my bogus asthma … It was Margaret [his wife] who insisted I couldn't die when the specialist said I must … But, think of it, they all went home that night and left me quite alone to face the crisis [he was in the Acland Hospital]. I was lightheaded & spent the hours in & out of some other world. Margaret was marvellously calm & by our side the old yeoman stock fought for us. To cut a damn long business short the old stock took the strain & got us through' …

Paul had been writing his autobiography *Outline*. 'My grandfather was a yeoman farmer whose family could be traced in a succession of uneventful Williams, Johns and Henrys to Henrie Nashe in the fifteenth century …' They farmed a hundred years at three places, Penn, Beaconsfield and Upton together with Langley. They began very humbly, I think. In a little Bible

of 1633 belonging to William and Eleanor Nash is this record
on ploughing –

Tew Eakrs is the first cast
Three Eakrs is the second cast
Three Eakrs is the Therd cast
Tew Eakres is the forth cast.

July, 1710 –

we had tew Eakres in the first cast
and tew Eakres in the second cast
and the Eakre in the Alder in the second cast
and tew Eakres in the therd cast
and the Eaker in the fearm in the therd cast
and tew Eakers in the forth cast
and the nex year it goes into the first cast

Stopped from flying because of his health, Paul released flowers
from their earth-bound stems. 'What the body is denied, the
mind must achieve.' He had been gardening.

'I had been breaking off the dying, dark, ethereal flowers of
a poisonous plant I had heard of [in John's *Poisonous Plants*,
1927?] when I heard – *Last night heavy and medium hellebores*
bombed the mountains of the Moon. You would think nothing
could be more straightforward. But when I came to assemble
my material – a full sheet of Cattermole paper (itself the
colour of a moonlight night) and the dried and pressed
hellebores and their seed pods (for the bombs), the plate of
the Moon's surface by Naysmith extracted from my second-
best book on the Heavens seemed to complete the corpus
apart from whatever drawing and painting was necessary ...
These small misadventures do not matter at all. The great

thing is to exercise constantly in the imaginings of aerial images, probing tentatively always, not unlike those incredibly brave engineers who go ahead of the infantry in search of mines – feeling for death at every foot. But it is death I have been writing about all the time ... Death, about which we are all thinking, death, I believe, is the only solution to this problem of how to be able to fly. Personally, I feel that if death can give us that, death will be good.'

Unknown to him his brother had filled the border below his sleeping head with vines – and hellebores. They are there still. Paul returned to Oxford the next morning and died a few weeks later, on 11th July.

When I visited his grave many years after this in Langley churchyard I discovered the sculpted motives which his wife had made from the emblems in Sir Thomas Browne's *Urne Buriall* – the owl, the broken architrave – were tangled in vetch and bramble, clover and fine grasses. I picked and pressed some of these plants for John. Dream flying manifested itself in two of the twentieth century's greatest paintings, Paul Nash's *Eclipse of the Sunflower* and *Solstice of the Sunflower*, Blake's poem

Ah, Sun-flower! weary of time,
Who countest the steps of the Sun

having grown 'gigantic' in his eyes.

'A few years later,' wrote Paul,

'in the course of making a series of drawings to illustrate Sir Thomas Browne's *Urne Buriall*, I came across the sentence referring to the soul visiting the Mansions of the Dead. This idea stirred my imagination deeply. I could see the emblem of the soul – a little winged creature, perhaps not unlike the ghost moth – perched upon the airy habitations of the skies... Although I made no more paintings of this kind, I exercised my prerogative of things in the sky if it suited my purpose ... Suddenly the sky was upon us all like a huge hawk, hovering, threatening ... I was hunting the sky for what I most dreaded ... It was a white flower. Ever since the Spanish civil war the idea of the *rose of death*, the name the Spaniards gave to the parachute, had haunted my mind, so that when war overtook us I strained my eyes always to see that dreadful miracle of the sky blossoming with these floating flowers. The first picture I made of the War was a collage of the Rose of Death. But it was not on the score of this prophetic fantasia that I was later, considerably to my surprise, appointed official war artist to the Air Ministry.'

John Nash in the studio at Bottengoms, 1961

FAMILY CIRCLES

JASPER CONTINUES TO CAST A LONG SHADOW ACROSS THE flint fields. He was an eclectic collector of Stone Age artefacts to bronze penny-in-the-slot machines from the old seaside, and anything in between. Immensely tall and fragile, always growing until his fine tousled head was far beyond us in more ways than one, his voice would descend in a run of rough barks. Myself being the only walker on the flint fields other than Jasper would watch him stalking the winter wheat, usually just after Christmas, a scavenger of Wormingford's Neolithic litter, every now and then giving his stork-like swoop when he suspected a find. For the worked and unworked stones could each be deceitfully alike until held in one's hand. On we would go, a long way apart, eyes down, Jasper filling his pockets with treasures, me picking up stuff which usually proved to be more plough-chipped than hand-chipped, and throwing it away. It was always dreadfully cold. And the rooks would kaaa-kaaa their way over us in black shoals.

At the farmhouse, and at any time of the year, Jasper would suddenly descend on me in search of company and priceless Huntley and Palmer's biscuit tins or 'that old wireless' or those

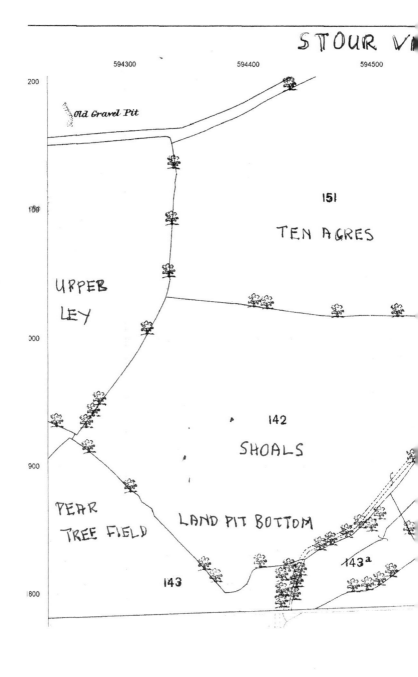

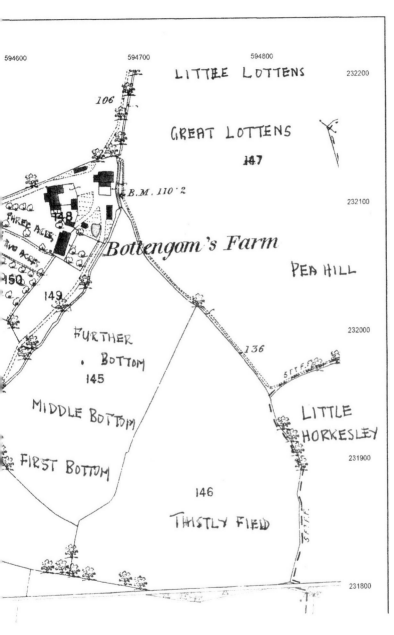

594600   594700   594800   232200

LITTLE LOTTENS

GREAT LOTTENS

147

106

232100

B.M. 110·2

THREE ACRES

148

TWO ACRES

Bottengom's Farm

PEA HILL

150

149

FURTHER

BOTTOM

145

136

5 FT F.P.

232000

MIDDLE BOTTOM

LITTLE

HORKESLEY

FIRST BOTTOM

231900

146

THISTLY FIELD

231800

Map of Bottengoms adapted by the author

old bottles with marble stoppers. His hoarder's gaze would alight on the yellow peony in full bloom. 'You can have a bit in the autumn, Jasper.' But as we would soon discover he could not wait. Where did I keep my old fork? He would bend his way through the low rooms, never banging his head, leaving a belated adolescent musk in his wake. Did I want that old clock? He could make it go. There would be a tender meeting with the ginger cat. Wound back into his dilapidated van, he would crash up the track.

It was in our Stone Age village by the Stour that Jasper's aloneness was most evident. Also his happiness. My only real find was a beautifully weighty palm-fitting gold-and-white stone which we both took to be a polishing tool or smoother. Jasper's loot was a very different matter. He arranged it in one of those handsome Victorian cabinets especially devised for a bird's-egg collection. Axes, arrows, flint saws, knives, beads, flint, everything nestled in a yellowing cotton wool. Never quite trustingly, he would place a particular treasure in my hand and then snatch it back like a child. And these brief exchanges would always make me imagine the original warm human hands of the ancient craftsmen. The archaeologists call the loop of the river which flows past the flint fields a meander. It was the River Meander which, changing course at Ephesus, left the harbour low and dry. The Stour meanders all the way from Cambridgeshire to the North Sea but at Wormingford a community turned its C into a D by sealing a meander with a linear cemetery of six ring-ditch graves. Jasper did not know this.

One lovely summer's day Jasper died. He was thirty-three. Never again the tall finders-keepers walker through our first settlement in the valley. Never again an eye like his for a find. I took his funeral at the Crem. 'Nothing religious', his family said.

And, 'No one will be there. Just us'. It was a burning noon and everyone aged thirty-three or thereabouts in our world was present. A multitude of upset young men and crying girls all dressed in shirts and jeans, all carrying skimpy flowers. I led them in. Jasper's absurdly long coffin swayed in my wake. Outside lay stone-filled acres, countless tombstones, miles of gravel, thousands of carved names and declarations of love, mossy hands, wings, chippings. The undertaker's cars were fiery chariots in the sunshine. It was all too hot for what had to be done. The elegant Crem man saw to it 'that I had everything'. During the Middle Ages it was presumed that we would all be aged thirty-three in heaven, the same age as Christ. As we passed up the aisle the Icelandic sculptor who lived in Penny's barn leant forward and placed a carved seagull on Jasper's feet. A woman strummed *Ave Maria* on a guitar and then, after the last notes had faded away, I told the sad crowd what most of them knew, but adding things like the walks in the winter fields to look for 'finds' and Jasper's jackdaw habits in, I supposed, all our houses. I then read one of those threnodies from the *Oxford Book of Greek Verse* which commemorate young men on whose stele, or thin stone monument, their laurels would hang until leaf by leaf they vanished. Euripides had written it ages after our flint princes whose circular tombs had sealed-off the river's meander, had existed. Having no knowledge of the wooden seagull, it seemed a small miracle of suitability.

> *Bird of the sea rocks, of the bursting spray,*
> *O halcyon bird,*
> *That wheelest crying, crying on thy way:*
> *Who knoweth grief can read the tale of thee:*
> *One love long lost, one song for ever heard …*

There is a small button beneath the Crem desk which brings the curtain down on a life. Jasper slid slowly from sight. Would this last movement disturb the seagull? It trembled but stayed with him. As most of the mourners were too young to know what a funeral was, the grief was terrible. They stood outside in the heat amidst the cellophane flowers, as much shocked as grief-stricken. Back in the village Jasper's parents and I walked by the lake to get over the jolt of it all, saying little. A mile or so down the lane the Stone-agers' bones were as usual ossifying with flint. It was calcium to chalk under the corn. 'That seagull!' said Jasper's mother, 'what a good touch'. I still have no idea what happened to him. At the time we called it 'outgrowing his strength'. This cannot have been right.

A long time after this, returning from the Bluebell Party at Tiger Hill in Tony's Range Rover, splashing across the stream as we used to do with our bikes and entering the village via the ford bridge, we heard a pistol shot and then the flap-flap-flap of a burst tyre. Doug and his lady happened to be passing. Joy lit up his face. 'A puncture!' For there is an indescribable pleasure in helping to change someone else's wheel – to being on the spot. 'And no wonder!' cried Doug, holding up a flint axehead. 'Come in handy at last!' When Tony ran his fingers along its edge, one of them bled. Doug repeated what luck it was for us that he happened to be passing and the axe trembled on the dashboard.

Aircraft fly over all the time. Those carrying a crowd fly high. The aerial photographers fly as low as they dare and hitting the long beams of the winter sun, their cameras combing the crops. The Suffolk and Essex Gliding Club saunters overhead. Also, a farmer from his private airstrip. All this once on Boxing Day or the Feast of Stephen. I thought of the young saint standing in the stoning pit and Paul the tentmaker guarding the clothes of the executioners, and behind them the city getting on with its normal business. Boulders, not flints, would have been thrown. We call our boulders 'sarsens', from Saracens, stranger stones, for they do not belong to our ecology. Too hard to cut into shape, they go into a church tower just as they are, or are humped to a garden as a kind of wonder. I have dragged one or two of them from where a ploughman has left them on a headland. Sarsens are hard blocks of tertiary sand, some a youthful pink having endured less than seventy million years of pressure. Unlike most oddities, they have no history of being unlucky. Just foreign. Once possessing a Lower and a Higher Stoney Field, my farmland must have often pulled out, like little Jack Horner, this plum of building material. Undetected like some ground iceberg, a plough could sail into one of them and get wrecked. The ploughmen called them, 'they bloody grut things'.

Paul Gilman, who looks after our Historic Environment Records at Chelmsford, has given me an Assessment Report by the Essex County Council Heritage Conservation Group called *A Cropmark Landscape in Three Dimensions*. I am enthralled. It stops all other reading for days. Holding it before me, I am able to stand exactly where the Neolithic and Bronze Age dead encircle one another in a kind of remote caring and intimacy. The earth-rings are linked in a line across the space left by the river's meander, enclosing a ritual ground. It is where Jasper picked up his best finds. So maybe also a barter market. Or even a thanksgiving place for the gift of flint. Holding *A Cropmark Landscape in Three Dimensions* in front of me like a kind of literary divining-rod, I note the shimmering river, the rising reeds, the mirrored clouds, the devoted swans and the deep silence. The wheat looks scanty but is well up and there could be a kingfisher. Brown dace swim against the current. In January the crop seems to grow on a beach, in March on a water-meadow. Sprayers will make tram-lines through it and these will become highways for historians.

It was the flint itself which the village harvested right up until the Great War. Bent low in family groups, women and children gathered it to mend the roads. They filled a pail and then a tumbril up to the chalk mark. The first school registers are furious with stone-picking absentees. The farmers were bewildered. When hadn't a child of eight been put out to work? None of the toilers were aware of the circles of the dead. They themselves were called the poor.

Ages would pass before further circles would be added to our landscape. Robert Morden was thirty-two when he published his map of Suffolk. It was covered with a rash of green spots, i.e. the parks of the nobility and gentry. Except for churches there was no other geographic information. No windmills, no herring-boats being blown along by Zephyrus and certainly no farms. Morden was an ambitious geographer who was aiming his map at the country-house where such industries had to be beyond the pale. Or out of sight. Not long after abbeys and priories became palaces a process of 'imparadising' began, which walled or fenced off farming and the peasantry in general. There was no rough husbandry in the Garden of Eden, just fruit trees and seed-bearing herbs, and a lovely river (the Euphrates). God walked in it in the evening to chat with his highest creation, Adam.

To 'impark' or enclose a country-house was a word first used in 1535. To call this house a 'seat' first appeared in 1607. Such dwellings became rural hubs of taste and learning, and local power-bases. Park-fences and brick walls ran for miles round them. They said that the latter could cost a pound a yard in the nineteenth century. A Suffolk feature is the serpentine or 'crinkle-crankle' wall. Fanciful lodges and gates flaring with heraldry permitted entrance to wonderful horticulture, architecture, music, 'society', local government and, often, the parish church. This having occupied the holy place since a Saxon cleared the wood to make the first field would still be adjacent to the mansion which now occupied the site of his wooden halle.

Most of Robert Morden's ringed worlds remain in situ although searching for a few of them will lead one to the ghostly grandeur of forsaken gardens and owl-visited ruins like the incomparably sad Houghton House in Bedfordshire, which was John Bunyan's House Beautiful. One finds them by the straight lines of World War Two airfields, these tell-tale fragments of pride driven into the concrete runways. At Stoke-by-Nayland, which I glimpse through the framework of oaks as I walk down the farm-track, and all of five miles distant, the medieval park remains but its hall has vanished. The youthful John Constable passed its miles of fence many times. The gamekeepers were

Track by a Pool by John Constable

instructed to 'Pray, permit Mr Constable to draw the trees' – a pass to a place where he did not belong. The hall-owners commissioned him to paint portraits of their houses and were angry when he included farm animals. His landscape with their agricultural contents were too 'low' for a gentleman's drawing-room and were not purchased. Having spent a fortune keeping the village out of sight one was hardly likely to hang views of it on one's walls. However, the student of agriculture might equally find a Constable questionable, for it was often an imparadising of what was happening to the workaday countryside, at that moment in starvation and ferment. Yet the great artist was not deceitful: as a boy he had witnessed farming harmony and prosperity in the Stour Valley, and his work was a declaration of how things should be. He watched the park-owners flee to their town-houses for safety, the stacks being fired and the labourers starving and rioting.

The map-maker's green rings are confident. They declare park-rule, park civilisation. They cluster for the most part in West Suffolk and the Blythings, a hundred to the north of the county. Great stretches of the county are parkless. The oddest thing about Morden's map is that many of the place-names are printed as they used to be pronounced and not as they are spelt. Laneham (Lavenham), Carsey (Kersey) etc. And all the time, not even the highest church tower being able to let one see a ring of graves in a field which grew flint, there existed below the surface of things communities which preceded the angels.

Park walls are an architecture in itself, and a vast undertaking. There are still lots of them to walk round both inside and out. Industrial revolution magnates continued to build them almost to the time of the First World War and the pinnacle of country-house culture. They support an entire brick or wooden fence natural history life of their own. Plants, insects, birds, creatures of every kind occupy them like an elongated abandoned city. Alec Clifton-Taylor says that all bricks were called 'waltyles' before the fifteenth century and he describes the ascendancy of the brick we know today. There are still two main bondings. The brick park wall, often running for miles around house and grounds, was for the most part a Georgian extravagance. Jane Austen comically exaggerated the bliss contained within them and the terrors which lay beyond them. In *Emma*, feeble Mr Woodhouse and his daughter not so much reside as reign. Their park wall would no doubt have been built in English garden wall bond (three or five courses of stretchers to one of headers) or in Flemish garden wall bond (three stretchers to one header in each course). Such a bonded circle would contain within it virtues, pleasures and feelings unknown to those without. It was said in Suffolk that they spared no expense.

It is quite a thought that in those days we might have a greater understanding of the society who made the ring-ditches by the river than that of which walled-out most of their village neighbours. Sir George Sitwell, staring across the whole of Sheffield from Renishaw, observed to his son, 'Do you realise, Osbert, that there is no one between us and the Locker-Lampsons?'

My stackyard was walled-in to stop the animals from getting out. A few yards remain. And here and there is a stout buttress supporting hanks of ivy. Tall nettles green the powdered mortar. I quarry it for rubble or nice hand-made edging bricks. Let tottering boundaries be. Our squire's hall is on high-ground and sheltered by trees. John Constable's Uncle Abram rented it for years. Our churchyard wall leans out, due, it is said, 'to the dead having a stretch'.

THE FLOWERS OF
MY FIELDS

Veronica Greenwood, RB and Richard Mabey, 1999

IN 1993 MY NEIGHBOUR MARY PERSUADED ME TO JOIN THE Wild Flower Society.

The following desirable and undesirable, and often hated plants are to be found in the cart-track, the stream, the orchard, the horse-ponds, fields, pastures, footpaths, woodland and garden faithfully most years. The Glory and 'the Rubbish'.

Acer campestre – Field Maple
Achillea – Millefolium – Yarrow
Aegopodium podagraria – Ground Elder
Aesculus hippocastanum – Horse Chestnut
Aethusa cynapium – Fool's parsley
Agrimonia eupatoria – Common Agrimony
Agrimonia procera – Fragrant Agrimony
Agrosta 'canina' – Velvet Bent
Agrosta capillaris – Fine Bent
Ajuga reptans – Common Bugle
Allium ursinum – Ramsons
Alopecurus geniculatus – Marsh Foxtail
Anemone nemorosa – Wood Anemone

Anthriscus sylvestris – Cow Parsley
Aphanes 'inexpectata' (microcarpa) – Slender Parsley Piert
Aquilegia vulgaris – Columbine
Arabis hirsuta – Hairy Rock-cress
Arctium minus – Lesser Burdock
Arrhenatherum elatius – False Oat-grass
Arum maculatum – Lords and Ladies – Cuckoo pint
Atropa bella-donna – Deadly Nightshade
Avena fatua – Wild Oat

Bellis perennis – Daisy
Borago officinalis – Borage
Bryonia dioica – White Bryony
Buddleja davidii – Buddleia

Caltha palustris – Marsh Marigold
Calystegia sepium – Hedge Bindweed
Calystegia silvatica – Large Bindweed
Campanula latifolia – Giant Bellflower
Cardamine flexuosa – Wavy Bitter-cress
Carex pendula – Drooping Sedge
Centaurea nigra – Common knapweed or hardhead
Centranthus rubra – Red Valerian
Ceratocapnos (Corydalis) Claviculata – Climbing Corydalis
Chaenorhinum minus – Small Toadflax
Chamaemelum nobile – Chamomile
Chelidonium majus – Greater Celandine
Chamerion (Epilobium) augustifolium – Rose-bay Willow-herb
Chenopodium album – Fat-hen
Chenopodium polyspermum – Many-seeded Goosefoot
Cichorium intybus – Chicory

Cirsium acaule – Dwarf Thistle
Cirsium arvense – Creeping Thistle
Claytonia (Montia) sibirica – Pink Purslane
Clematis vitalba – Traveller's Joy – Old Man's Beard
Colchicum autumnale – Meadow Saffron
Convallaris majalis – Lily-of-the-Valley
Convolvulus arvensis – Field Bindweed
Cornus sanguinea – Dogwood
Corylus avellana – Hazel
Cotoneaster horizontalis – Wallspray. Fishbone Cotoneaster
Crataegus laevigata – Woodland or Midland Hawthorn
Crataegus monogyna – Common Hawthorn
Crepis-capillaris – Smooth Hawk's-beard
Cymbalaria muralis – Ivy-leaved Toadflax

Meadow Saffron, wood
engraving by John Nash
from *Poisonous Plants:
Deadly, Dangerous and Suspect*
(Etchells and Macdonald,
1927)

Dactylis glomerata – Cock's-foot
Daphne laureola – Spurge Laurel
Deschampsia cespitosa – Tufted Hair-grass
Digitalis purpurea – Foxglove
Dryopteris affinis – Golden-scaled Male Fern

Epilobium hirsutum – Great Willow-herb
Equisetum arvense – Common Horsetail
Equisetum telmateia – Great Horsetail
Eryngium maritimum – Sea-holly
Euphorbia amygdaloides – Wood-spurge
Euphorbia lathyris – Caper-spurge

Fallopia sachalinensis – Giant Knotweed
Festuca elatior – Tall Fescue
Foeniculum vulgare – Fennel
Fraxinus excelsior – Ash
Fritillaria meleagris – Fritillary

Galanthus nivalis – Snowdrop
Galeopsis speciosa – Large Hemp-nettle
Galeospsis tetrahit – Common Hemp-nettle
Galium aparine – Goose-grass. Cleavers
Galium verum – Lady's Bedstraw
Geranium dissectum – Cutleaved Cranesbill
Geranium pratense – Meadow Cranesbill
Geranium robertianum – Herb Robert
Geranium sanguineum Bloody Cranesbill
Geum urbanum – Herb Bennet
Glechoma hederacea – Ground Ivy

Hedera helix – Ivy
Helictotrichon (Avenula) pratense – Meadow Oat-grass
Helleborus foetidus – Stinking Hellebore
Helleborus viridus – Green Hellebore
Heracleum mantegazzianum – Giant Hogweed
Hieracium murorum – Hawkweed
Hippuris vulgaris – Mare's-tail
Holcus lanatus – Yorkshire Fog
Hordeum secalinum – Meadow Barley
Humulus lupulus – Hop
Hyacinthoides non-scriptus – Bluebell
Hypericum androsaemum – Tutsan
Hypercium perforatum – Common St John's-wort
Hypochaeris radicata – Common cat's-ear

Helleborus foetidus,
wood engraving by
John Nash, 1927

Ilex aquifolium – Holly
Impatiens glandulifera – Himalayan Balsam
Iris foetidissima – Stinking Iris
Iris pseudacorus – Yellow Flag

Lamiastrum galeobdolon – Yellow Archangel
Lamium album – White Dead-nettle
Lamium maculatum – Spotted Dead-nettle
Lamium purpureum – Red Dead-nettle
Lapsana communis – Nipplewort
Lathyrus pratensis – Meadow Vetchling
Lepidium campestre – Field Pepperwort
Lithospermum officinale – Common Gromwell
Lolium perenne – Perennial Rye Grass
Lonicera periclymenum – Honeysuckle

Malus sylvestris – Crab Apple
Malva neglecta – Dwarf Mallow
Malva sylvestris – Common Mallow
Meconopsis cambrica – Welsh Poppy
Medicago lupulina – Black Medick
Medicago sativa – Lucerne
Meum athamanticum – Spignel
Milium effusum – Wood Millet
Myosotis arvensis – Common Forget-me-not
Myostis ramosissima – Early Forget-me-not
Myrrhis odorata – Sweet Cicely

Narcissus 'pseudonarcissus' – Wild Daffodil

Onobrychis viciifolia – Sanfoin

Origanum vulgare – Marjoram

Ornithogalam augistifolium (umbellatum) – Common Star of
   Bethlehem

Oxalis acetosella – Wood Sorrel

Papaver dubium – Long-headed Poppy

Papaver rhoeas – Corn Poppy

Pentaglottis sempervirens – Green Alkanet

Persicaria bistorta – Common Bistort

Persicaria lapathifolia – Pale Persicaria

Petacites hybridus – Common Butterbur

Phalaris arundinacea – Reed Grass

Phyllitis scolopendrium – Hart's Tongue

Picris echioides – Bristly Ox-tongue

Plantago major – Rat's-tail or Greater Plantain

Poa nemoralis – Wood Meadow-grass

Poa Pratensis – Smooth Meadow-grass

Polygala serpyllfollia – Heath Milkwort

Polygala vulgaris – Common Milkwort

Populus tremula – Aspen

Potentilla anserina – Silverweed

Potentilla reptans – Creeping Cinquefoil

Primula acaulis vulgaris – Primrose

Primula veris – Cowslip

Prunus domestica – Wild Plum

Prunus spinosa – Blackthorn

Pseudofumaria (Corydalis) lutea – Yellow Corydalis

Pteridium aquilinum – Bracken

Autumn, wood engraving by John Nash for H.E. Bates'
Flowers and Faces (Golden Cockerel Press, 1935)

Quercus robur – Pendunculate Oak

Ranunculus acris – Meadow Buttercup
Ranunculus auricomus – Wood Goldilocks
Ranunculus bulbosus – Bulbous Buttercup
Ranunculus ficaria – Lesser Celandine
Ranunculus peltatus – Pond Water Crowfoot
Ranunculus sardous – Hairy Buttercup
Rhamnus cathartica – Common Buckthorn
Rhinanthus minor – Yellow Rattle
Ribes rubrum – Red Currant
Ribes uva crispa – Gooseberry
Rosa canina – Dog Rose
Rubus fruticosus – Bramble
Rumex acetosa – Common Sorrel
Rumex obtusifolius – Broad-leaved Dock
Ruscus aculeatus – Butcher's Broom

Salix caprea – Goat Willow
Salix cinerea – Grey Willow
Salix fragilis – Crack Willow
Salvia verbenaca – Clary
Sambucus nigra – Common Elder
Senecio jacobaea – Common Ragwort
Senecio vulgaris – Groundsel
Silene dioica – Red Campion
Silene latifolia – White Campion
Silybum marianum – Milk Thistle
Solanum nigrum – Black Nightshade
Sonchus asper – Prickly Sow Thistle
Sonchus oleraceus – Smooth Sow Thistle

Stachys arvensis – Field Woundwort
Stachys sylvatica – Hedge Woundwort
Symphoricarpos albus – Snowberry
Symphytum officinale – Common Comfrey

Tanacetum vulgare – Tansy
Taraxacum 'officianale' – Dandelion
Taxus baccata – Yew
Teesdalia nudicaulis – Shepherd's Cress
Tragopogon pratensis – Goat's Beard
Trifolium dubium – Common Yellow Trefoil
Trifolium repens – White Clover

Urtica dioica – Stinging Nettle

Veronica filiformis – Slender Speedwell
Veronica hederifolia – Ivy-leaved Speedwell
Veronica persica – Common Field Speedwell
Viburnum opulus – Guelder Rose
Vicia cracca – Tufted Vetch

Looking again at this list, made according to the rules of the Wild Flower Society some time past, kept strictly from March to October each year, I suddenly saw it in small farm terms and not botanically. And what a difference. And there was myself, a Suffolk boy and one of the last to weed fields for pennies. And there was John Clare in the Blue Bell with his pockets straggling with fritilleries or some such treasure. And, briefly, it was all of a piece, his weedy world and mine. Bent backs, not sprays. Clare saw glory in the ruts, his fellow labourers saw 'the rubbish'. To know its real names, he believed, would be an enlightenment,

Antique Flowers, line drawing by John Nash for Jason Hill's
The Curious Gardener (Faber and Faber, 1932)

would illuminate their existence. They laughed. He called them 'clowns' – boors. But they were selective, adoring the primrose, using the herbs, though hating the unmanageable 'growth'. Cleaning the summer fields and ditches was for them the agricultural equivalent of Canute's command to the sea. The bliss when poisons stopped the annual green tide!

Bottengoms Farm, which ceased to exist after the 1920s, knew hand-weeding alone. Not until its acres seeped into the surrounding land would they be chemically cleansed. When the Big Field, which had been half a dozen of the old fields, was set-aside, I combed it for maybe old and rare corn plants but found that it was peopled by thugs. Lots of plough-split flints and some saplings making the most of the rest from crops. Where possible the weeds were kept under by the weak, women, children and the aged. Strong men had other work to do. Weeders toiled for pittances. 'How it rained! How it shone!'

Mr Stovin, a Lincolnshire farmer in the 1870s, says it all. He could have been saying it about Bottengoms. And he was saying it as English agriculture was about to be washed away, although he could not know this.

'How dark and gloomy the prospects! How thick and hazy the air! How leaden the skies! Yesterday I was pulling ketlocks out of the turnips, also neadles, redrobbin and scarlet poppies. It is a proverb that weeds grow apace. Experience brings home the truth. There is not a weed growing in my turnip fields but will come to maturity and yield its thousandthfold increase many months before the turnip itself. What a tenacious hold they have upon our soil. If we ease our vigilance they soon become predominant. A skilful and persevering hand is required to maintain empire over this department of natural laws and forces... It is defiant in its hardiness and rampant in its march to maturity. Neither flood nor drought can jeopardise its produce. Even though torn up by its roots and cast out a thousand times over, phoenix-like it obtains resurrection from its own ashes. What a tyranny has been exercised over man by the thistle ... The great contest which constitutes one portion of the battle of the farmer's life is with the organised and vital rubbish.'

As it rained Mr Stovin observed that 'All nature looked skattern and forlorn.'

Twitch and docks might be pulled about in a useless human fashion but were virtually immovable. Twitch was partly dragged out by a spiked wooden cart with a harrow on top, using a horse, and docks have been found growing downwards rather than die. A Norfolk farmer despaired over the tenacity of docks. 'Even a bacillus knows where to stop, for the Black Death was satisfied with killing half the population'. Docks are few and far between at Bottengoms. They are meadow-wreckers.

When farm weeding is treated as a normal non-irritating task, as Dorothy Hartley does in her peerless *Lost Country Life*, it becomes as interesting as fruit-picking. One might even botanise whilst doing it and not be a clown. It is not without some of the beauty of the harvest itself.

'Unless the corn had been harrowed, till weeding began the only rows in a cornfield were made by the seed rolling into the plough furrows. Now along these rows walks the weeder. He uses two sticks: with the first, hooked stick he plucks the weed out from among the corn stalks, and with the second, forked stick, pins the weed's head down under the fork. The weeder then steps one pace forward, placing his foot on the head of the weed, and, with this forward movement, swings the hooked stick behind him, lifting the root of the weed high out of the ground, before dropping it in line. In this way each pulled-up weed is shaken clear of the soil, and laid with its root over the buried head of the previous weed. Thus, as the weeder goes along the line of the furrows he lays a mulch of decaying weeds alongside the roots of the corn, and forms a line between the rows at least as wide as a foot. Weeding employed a definite rhythm, and the feet of the weeder formed the lines on which much of the weeder's work depended. Weeding continued steadily till the workers were called away to haymaking. The only weed that was not uprooted was bindweed on corn in the ear, as pulling that out shed the corn so badly it was better to cut the stem low down and let it be threshed later.'

As the great rains beat down on Britain in the 1870s, washing corn and weeds into one another, washing the labourers onto the railways and into the colonies, the young Thomas Hardy wrote a novel in which gorse and ling destroyed the reasonable expectancy of a community. Egdon Heath clamped down on it. Egdon was, he fancied, Lear's remorseless heath. We walk and preserve such places in wonder and delight, being far from clowns.

SIR
CEDRIC
MORRIS
Artist
Plantsman
1889-1982

Sir Cedric Morris's grave, photographed by RB. His pupil Beth Chatto
grew the flowers. His friend Donald Simpson lettered the Welsh slate.
I said a few words. All this in Hadleigh Cemetery. His lifelong companion
Lett Haines lies nearby.

June, Nine p.m.

The social bees work late,
Barren girls with honeyed thighs
Labouring among aquilegia,
The eagle flower, purple-spurred,
Multitudinous, nearly a weed.

I sit in the mid-year garden
To hear the poplars clatter,
And to admire what I have done.
The day is advanced, the bees
Drone vespers, the sun hits the wheat.

Farmers sat on the doorstep
At this hour, aching and comfortable,
Their eyes registering
A patch of pinks and mignonette
As their gaze settled for the big field.

An ancient man who had been
Young here arrived to say,
'Mother saw to the flowers, of course'.
Of course. Father saw to that.
Their ancient son spoke of hives,

Hives here? 'Hives, honeybees,
Pears in the orchard, muck
In the soil, all you had to have.'
The same water plashing, as
They put it then, and gulped by the horses.

Their shoes turn up in the beds.
I see my luckless father
Ploughing, confident in his rut,
His eye on the holly marker,
His tongue conversing with beasts,

Social bees will not pause
While there is light, while an anther
Can be seen to yield. And the poplars
Applaud them with grey and silver leaves,
The roses blacken, the cornfield fades.

The Farmhouse Window, pen-and-ink drawing by John Nash, 1958

October, line drawing by John Nash from John Pudney's *Almanack of Hope*
(John Lane, 1944)

BIBLIOGRAPHY

Barrett, Hugh. *Early to Rise: A Suffolk Morning*, Faber and Faber, 1967

Beaumont, Winifred and Taylor, Ann. *Wormingford: An English Village*, 1960

Bell, Adrian. *Men and the Fields*, Batsford, 1939

Clifton-Taylor, Alec. *The Pattern of English Building*, Faber and Faber, 1972

Cullyer, John. *The Gentleman and Farmer's Assistant*, 1798

Hartley, Dorothy. *Lost Country Life*, Pantheon, 1979

Higham, T. F. and Bowra, C. M. *The Oxford Book of Greek Verse in Translation*, Oxford University Press, 1938

Nash, Paul. *Outline*, Faber and Faber, 1949

Stovin, Jean (ed.). *Journals of a Methodist Farmer 1871–1875*, Croom Helm, 1982

Strachan, D., Brown, N. and Knopp, D. *The Stour Valley Project: A Cropmark Landscape in Three Dimensions*, Essex County Council, 2000

Sturt, Neville (ed.). *The Marriage Register of Wormingford*, Phillimore's Parish Register Series

White, Andrew. *The Lost Tudor Hunting Lodge at Wormingford*, Colchester Archaeological Group, 2010

Whitehead, R. A. *Garrett's of Leiston*, Marshall, 1964

INDEX

Arger Fen, 74
Assassin, The, 15
Austen, Jane, 22, 103

Barrett, Hugh, 29
Barrett, Roderic, 32
Bell, Adrian, 79
Benton End, 13, 15
Beresford-Jones, Mary, 107
Blake, William, 89
Bloomsbury, 16
Blythe, George, 16
Blythe, Matilda, 16
Bottengoms Farm, 15, 22, 24, 28, 32,
   33, 35, 39, 47, 49, 50, 57, 63, 70,
   72, 80, 118, 119
Bottomley, Gordon, 87
Browne, Sir Thomas, 89
Buckinghamshire, 82
Bunyan, John, 101

Carrington, Dora, 82
Castle Hedingham, 76
Charles I, Clothiers' Petition to, 47
Chatto, Beth, 121
Civil War, 48
Clare, John, 35, 116
Cobbett, William, 15
Cohu, William, 25
Colchester, 32, 87
Constable, John, 26, 32, 50, 101, 102, 103
Cornwall, 17
Cotswolds, 47
Crabbe, George, 55
Cranbrook, Jock, 75
Cullyer, John, 49

de Bures, Sir Robert, 17
Dedham, 47
Douglas, Keith, 76
Dowsing, William, 48

East Anglia, 39
East Anglian School of Drawing
   and Painting, 13
East Anglian Wool Trade, 47
East Bergholt, 50
Edmunds, Robert, 56
Elizabeth I, 63–76
Elmy, Mrs, 55
Euripides, 97

Flaherty, Robert, 32
Freud, Lucien, 15

Gallipoli, 16
Garnon's (Gernon's), 22
George, St, 22
Gilman, Paul, 99
Gilpin, William, 25
Girling, Richard, 50
Godly People of the Stour Valley, 48
Gower, 17
Great Glemham, 32

Hadleigh, 13
Haines, Lett, 13, 121
Hambling, Maggi, 15
Hardy, Thomas, 9, 33, 57, 120
Hartley, Dorothy, 35, 119
Hartley, L.P., 84
Hazlitt, William, 13
Henry VIII, 76

James I, 64
James, Henry, 84

Kühlenthal (Nash), Christine, 41, 80,
82, 84, 86

Langham, 47
Lavenham, 49, 102
Lawrence of Arabia, film, 69
Lewis, Herbert, 40

Mary, Queen of Scots, 71
Mary Rose, 33
Massachusetts, 47, 49
Mitchell, Alan, 25
Morden, Robert, 100, 101, 102
Morris, Sir Cedric 13, 14, 36, 121
Mozart, W.A. 13
Munson, Harry, 40

Nash, John, 13, 40, 41, 51, 57, 58, 70, 75,
79–88, 90
Nash, Margaret (Bunty), 85, 87
Nash, Paul, 58, 85–89
Nash, William and Eleanor, 88
Nayland, 80
New England, 49
North Essex and West Suffolk Hunt, 71

Oxford, Earl of, 76

Parker, Rowland, *The Common Stream*, 15
Peake, Mervyn, 40

Pleasants, Mrs, 16
Pearce, Jasper, 91–99

Ravilious, Eric, 82, 83

Saunders, Doug, 98
Shakespeare, William, 76
Simpson, Donald, 121
Sitwell, Sir George, 103
Smallbridge, 69, 71, 73
Stoke-by-Nayland, 101
Stour, River, 21, 22, 28, 47, 48, 69,
75, 96, 102
Strong, Sir Roy, 72
Suffolk, 32, 47, 100, 103, 116
Suffolk, horses, 30

Tiger Hill, 74, 98
Titian, 71, 72
Turner, James, 13
Tyley, Tony, 98

Vautor, Thomas, 72

Waldegrave, Sir William, 22, 70, 71
White, Gilbert, 24
Wild Flower Society, 107
Winthrop, John, 49
Wolsey, Thomas, 24
Wormingford, Widermund, 22, 25,
69, 70, 74, 93, 96

Yggdrassil, 25